QUILTING

Activities for Young Learners

15 Easy and Delightful "No-Sew" Projects
That Reinforce Early Skills & Concepts

by Christy Hale

New York • Toronto • London • Auckland • Sydney
Mexico City • New Delhi • Hong Kong • Buenos Aires

Teaching *Resources*

For my dear friends
Jeannie Hutchins and Margaret Marcy Emerson,
who both patch beautiful patterns
out of life's diverse scraps. —C.H.

Interior design and illustration by Christy Hale

ISBN: 0-439-43463-7
Copyright © 2005 by Christy Hale
Published by Scholastic Inc.
All rights reserved.
Printed in the U.S.A.

1 2 3 4 5 6 7 8 9 10   40   13 12 11 10 09 08 07 06 05

CONTENTS

ABOUT THIS BOOK

Quilts are loaded with personal and communal meanings. They can link us to our own personal histories or our shared experiences. At best, they do both!

Why do quilt projects with young children? In early childhood, children are making the transition from "me" to "us." By age five, most children are developmentally ready to begin seeing things from another person's point of view. Joining a group is an opportunity to learn responsibility—each group member pulls his or her own weight. Using quilt projects in the classroom can build a sense of unity within a group. Children begin to see that artists are not necessarily independent, isolated individuals; rather, they can be interdependent, vital parts of a collaborative process. With quilt projects, each child's contribution is essential to the completed structure!

This book is filled with simple ideas in a variety of media. You'll find quilts involving painting, printing, rubbing, weaving, cutting, constructing, and sculpting—all designed to develop fine-motor control and hand-eye coordination. All the materials are easily available. Projects link to a variety of themes: patterns, night and day, seasons, neighborhood, other cultures, holidays, and even recycling. You'll enjoy seeing children's explorations come together in dazzling displays!

You can plan these quilt projects to tie into your curriculum. Quilts can help teach math, social studies, design concepts, and more—all at the same time! You'll find related books listed for each project, to be used as introductions or extensions to the project. And, an eight-page color insert lets you see each completed project.

You'll want to display the completed and assembled quilt in a prominent location so that you can discuss the final work and the process. Extend your project with poems, journal entries, art reviews and critiques, or even an art opening!

Remember, "The whole is greater than the sum of its parts!"

Materials

Recycle! Scavenge! Most supplies necessary for these projects are free for the taking. You might send home letters to families enlisting contributions (see page 52), or post the following list on your classroom door:

- Construction paper scraps
- Magazines & newspapers
- Manila folders & envelopes
- Business envelopes with printed patterned interiors
- Shoeboxes
- Paper towel rolls
- Egg cartons
- Twist-ties
- Cardboard scraps
- Styrofoam trays & packing "peanuts"
- Leaves
- String
- Buttons
- Keys

Setting Up

These projects require very little set-up. You'll want to gather the materials in advance, and precut all pieces (you can store them in resealable bags). Some more helpful hints:

- Use recycled Styrofoam trays for paints and inks.
- Have child-safe scissors and other necessary tools available.
- Have children wear smocks or aprons.
- Have moist towelettes available for easy hand washing.
- Create stations where small groups can work. Cover tables in newspaper for easy clean up. Enlist an adult helper to supervise each station and provide assistance.

Assembling the Quilts

The projects in this book can be created with fabric or paper squares. If you ora classroom volunteer have sewing skills, give fabric a try—otherwise, paper squares are a simple and satisfying alternative!

For Fabric Squares

Allow ½" for all seams. Sew squares directly together. Or, try a windowpane construction, which features contrasting narrow fabric strips separating the quilt blocks. Simply cut contrasting colored cloth rectangles the length of the squares, but only one third the width. Alternate sewing squares and rectangles.

For Paper Squares

Use adhesive to attach squares to a poster board, or staple directly to your bulletin board. You can simulate a windowpane construction by separating the squares and leaving spaces between them to show a contrasting colored background paper.

Squares can be sewn or taped directly together.

Squares can be sewn together with strips of fabric, or stapled to a bulletin board with a paper background.

Talking to Children About Art

Here are some conversation starters you might try as you observe children's work.

- I notice you are using a lot of (name of color). What made you choose this color? What does it remind you of?

- This part of your work looks (description such as rippled, soft, bumpy, bright). How did you create that effect?

- I see you're using a (name of tool, such as sponge). How is that different from using a (another tool, such as paintbrush)?

- I see you're using a (name of medium, such as newsprint). How is that different from using a (another medium, such as heavier paper)?

- What would you like to call your work?

- When you look at everyone's work together, what do you see? What is the same? What is different?

Art Talk!

In these boxes you'll find definitions of art-related terms for your own reference. Though naturally you wouldn't use some of these words when talking directly to children, they explain the underlying concepts of each activity. For instance, even though a child would not understand "abstract expressionism," he or she would be able to see that painting with string makes a silly picture that does not necessarily look like an object. Many of these terms, however, such as *line* or *pattern*, are appropriate for use in conversation with children. See page 61 for a glossary of all the terms.

Meeting the Early Childhood Standards

The activities in this book align with the guidelines and teaching practices recommended by the national standards as summarized by McRel (Mid-continent Research for Education and Learning) and National Association for the Education of Young Children (NAEYC).

McRel Visual Arts Standards (4th Ed.) for Kindergarten **Children:**
- Understand and apply media, techniques, and processes related to the visual arts
- Know how to use structures (sensory qualities, organizational principles, expressive features) and functions of art
- Know a range of subject matter, symbols, and potential ideas in the visual arts
- Understand the visual arts in relation to history and cultures

- Understand the characteristics and merits of one's own artwork and the artwork of others

In *Can You See What I See? Cultivating Self-Expression Through Art* (2004), NAEYC states:

Over the years, educators, psychologists, and philosophers have come to appreciate the value of children's art and its important role in early childhood education. It is now agreed by many in the field that exploring and creating with art materials helps children become more sensitive to the physical environment (for instance, shape, size, and color); promotes cognitive development (decision-making, nonverbal communication, and problem solving); and increases their social and emotional development (accomplishment, individuality, independence, autonomy, appreciation of others' work, and sharing).

Source: *Content Knowledge: A Compendium of Standards and Benchmarks for K–12 Education* (4th ed.) Mid-continent Research for Education and Learning, 2004.

Quilting Bees

Quilting has a long history, with examples found in many countries and cultures. In America, the "patchwork" quilt was born from necessity. Because early settlers had limited resources and could not afford European cloth, they became great recyclers, cutting apart worn-out garments and reusing the scraps. Bits of garments of all fabric types, ribbons, and trims were pieced into patchwork bedding. Neighbors traded scraps to give variety to piece-work. In addition, when fabric was bought off the bolt at the general store, the selection was the same for everyone locally. Exchanging portions of these fabrics created more possiblities for unique patchwork. This swapping of resources led to a sharing of labor in the pinning, basting, and stitching of the tops, and the quilting bee was born!

A "bee" means people gathering for a special purpose. A group of eight could sit around a quilting frame and stitch the top of a quilt together; their collaborative effort would speed the task along. This social event was a break in the loneliness of isolated pioneers. Usually the bee would last all day, people taking turns quilting while others cooked up supper. News, recipes, tips, and support were in abundance. In the evening there was feasting, singing, dancing, and courting.

Try a modern quilting bee in your classroom!

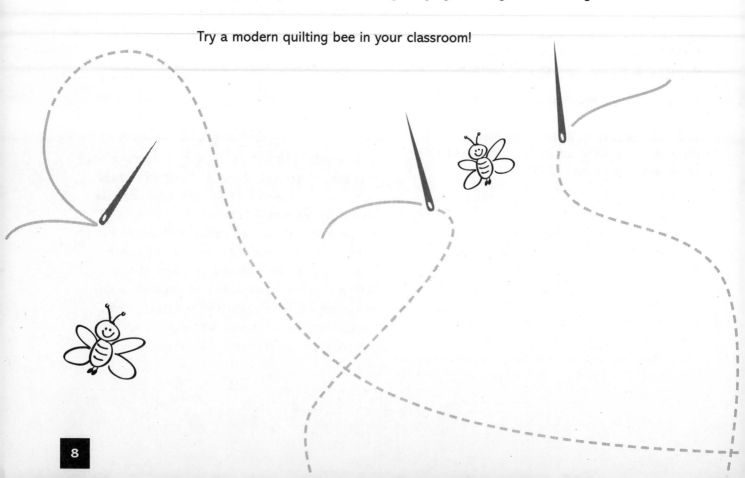

Organizing Your Own Class Bee

Gather the energy in your class, school, or district and create commemorative quilts, fund-raising auction quilts, or quilts for the charity of your choice. Use quilts to retell a story, to highlight an area of study, to celebrate a season or holiday, or to express friendship. A "bee" with families or even another class is a perfect opportunity to build class community.

1 Arrange a date, time, and gathering place with a large work area.

2 Select a theme. Purchase or collect the required materials. Prepare templates.

3 Package materials, templates, and instructions for making each block.

4 Send out invitations and organize volunteers to bring refreshments.

5 At the bee, hand out packets and work on quilt squares.

6 Have an adult piece the squares together into the final quilt!

STRING ART QUILT

Here's a great way to introduce a study of lines. You'll end up with a beautiful abstract expressionist quilt!

Materials

- 7-inch cloth or paper squares in different colors, one per child
- Tempera paints for paper or textile paints for cloth
- Shallow containers for paint (bowls, plates or Styrofoam trays)
- Thick string cut in different length (up to 10 inches)
- Beads with holes large enough to thread string

How-to

1 Divide the class into small groups. Provide each group with shallow containers of paint, several pieces of string with beads tied to the ends for easy handling, and cloth or paper squares. (You might plan a limited color palette to celebrate a special holiday, mark a season, or teach about color families.)

2 Show children how to hold the bead, dip the string into the paint, and gently press it into the paint to coat it with color. Have children use a separate piece of string for each color of paint.

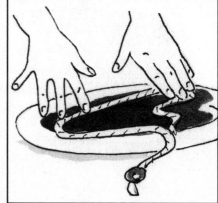

3 Have children lift the string from the paint and place it on the square, allowing the string to curve and twist naturally. Show them how to press firmly with fingertips along the string's path, making a print on their squares. They then lift the string off and repeat the process again and again with different colors.

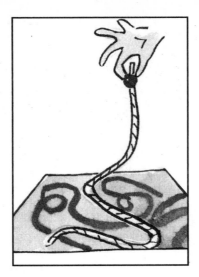

4 Allow the paint on the squares to dry completely. (If you are using textile paint and cloth, let the paint dry and then iron the reverse side of the cloth to heat-set the textile ink, making it permanent.)

5 Assemble squares to form a quilt (see page 6). Gather around the assembled quilt and ask children to describe the lines they see (*thick, thin, short, long, wavy, zigzag, straight,* and so on).

Book Links

Action Jackson by Jan Greenberg and Sandra Jordon (Millbrook, 2002)
Takes a close look at Pollock's life while he creates a major painting. A great introduction to this abstract kinetic artist!

Jackson Pollock: Getting to Know the World's Greatest Artists by Mike Venezia (Children's Press, 1994)
Uses words, comics, and paintings to explain the personal style of this contemporary American painter.

Lines by Philip Yenawine (The Museum of Modern Art, 1991)
Using reproductions of art from the museum collection, the author explores artists' uses of line in painting.

Art Talk!

Abstract Expressionism is a style in which the artist expresses a feeling or idea with form, line, or color, without having a representational subject matter.

Line is the path of a moving point through space, or a continuous mark. It can vary by length, width, texture, direction, and curve.

Movement refers to the path the viewer's eye takes through the artwork. It can be directed along lines, edges, shapes, and colors within the artwork.

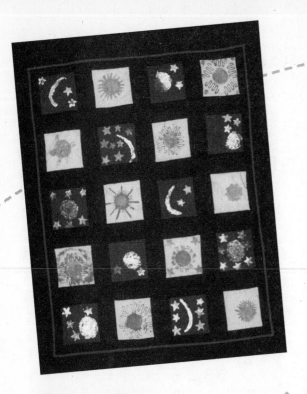

SUN, MOON & STARS QUILT

Print with fruits, vegetables, and kitchen tools, and transform the common into the celestial!

Materials

- **7-inch cotton cloth or paper squares in deep blue and yellow, one of each per child**
- **Yellow, orange, and white water-based printing ink or tempera paints for paper, or yellow, orange, and opaque white textile paints for cloth**
- **Shallow containers for paint or ink**
- **Fruits and vegetables for printmaking (starfruits, cabbages, acorn squash, plantains, grapefruit, onions)**
- **Forks**
- **Potato mashers**

How-to

1 Ask children to describe the shapes the moon makes. Share one of the books listed on page 14 and discuss the phases of the moon: crescent, quarter, gibbous, full, and so on. Ask, *Does the sun also appear to change shape?* (no) Explain that children will be creating pictures of the sun, moon, and stars.

2 Demonstrate how to make a stamp print. Take a fruit, vegetable, or utensil, and press it into the container of ink or tempera paint. Then stamp it onto the cloth or paper, transferring the color onto that surface.

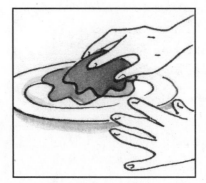

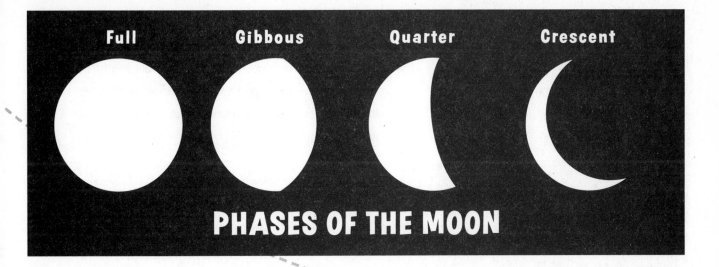

PHASES OF THE MOON

Full　　Gibbous　　Quarter　　Crescent

3 For larger items such as plantain, acorn squash, and cabbage, show how to paint a thin layer of ink or paint over the surface of the fruit or vegetable. Take the newly "loaded" fruit or vegetable and press it onto the cloth or paper quilt square.

4 Set up different work areas as either "day" or "night" stations. Provide "day" stations with yellow cloth or paper squares, orange printing ink, acorn squash, onions, and grapefruits (all cut in half), forks, and potato mashers. Stock the "night" stations with deep blue cloth or paper squares, yellow or white printing ink, starfruits (cut in half to reveal a flat star), cabbages and grapefruits (also halved), and plantains (uncut).

Day Square

5 Encourage children to experiment at each station. At the "day" station, have children use acorn squash, onions, or grapefruits to print orange suns on the yellow squares. Show them how forks or potato mashers can be used to make lines radiating from the center!

6 At the "night" station, watch children discover how a printed plantain makes a crescent moon! A printed cabbage texture resembles craters on the moon. When a cabbage is partially inked and printed, it creates a half moon. A printed grapefruit looks like a full moon. Starfruits print five-pointed stars! Each child can fill a blue square with any combination of nighttime images.

Night Square

Book Links

The Birth of the Moon by Coby Hol
(North South Books, 2000)
This sweet, simple picture book introduces
very young children to the waxing and
waning of the moon.

The Moon Seems to Change by Barbara
Emberley (HarperTrophy, 1987)
Demonstrates the phenomena of the
moon's phases with an an orange, pencil,
and flashlight.

Print Making by Michael Pell
(Book Sales, 1995)
This book introduces children to the
basic aspects of printmaking. Includes
a project guide with a variety of ideas
and methods.

So That's How the Moon Changes Shape
by Allan Fowler, (Children's Press, 1991)
A great nonfiction photo book about
the moon and why it changes shape
throughout the month.

The Sun Is Always Shining Somewhere
by Allan Fowler, (Children's Press, 1992)
A good introduction to studying the sun,
answering common questions: Why is
there a night and day? Why is the sun a
star? Why does it look so much bigger
than other stars?

7 After each child has printed one day square and one night square, allow paint to dry completely. (If you are using textile ink and cloth, allow the ink to dry completely then iron the reverse side of the cloth to heat-set the ink, making it permanent.) Assemble the squares, alternating yellow and blue, to form a quilt (see page 6).

8 Copy the color wheel on page 15. Post it and color it in with crayons as children watch. Ask children, *Which colors seem "cool" and which seem "warm"? Which is usually cooler, day or night?* Compare the colors in the quilt to those on the wheel (See "Art Talk!" below).

Art Talk!

Cool colors
On one half of the color wheel are the "cool colors," from green to blue to violet.

Warm colors
On the other half of the color wheel are the "warm colors," from yellow to orange to red.

Color Wheel

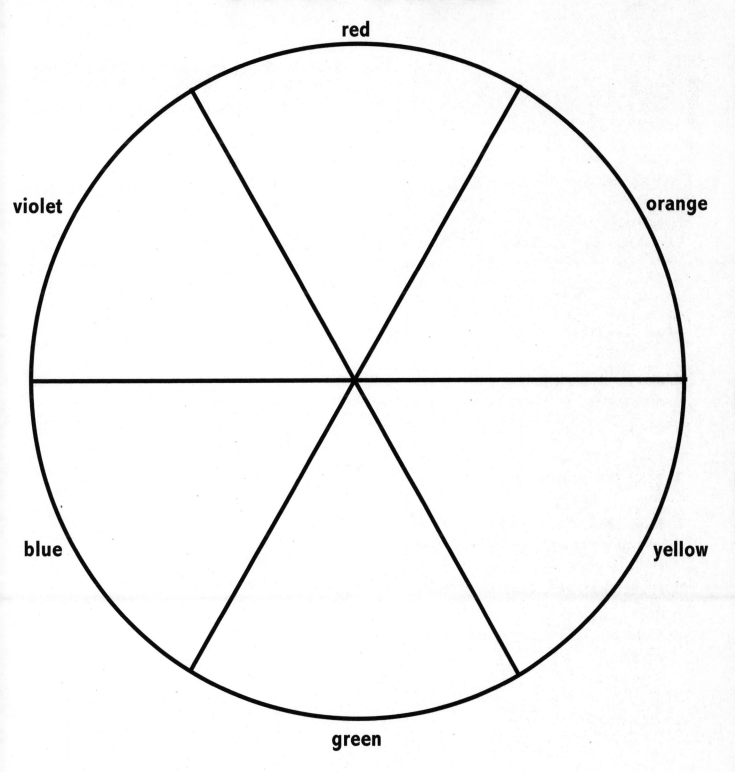

red

violet

orange

blue

yellow

green

LEAF PRINT QUILT

Celebrate the beauty of seasons, the diversity of leaf shapes, and the beauty of leaf structures with this easy printing project.

Materials

- Bags for collecting leaves, one per child
- Leaves
- Waxed paper
- 7-inch cloth or paper squares in different colors
- Textile paints or water-based printing ink for cloth or tempera paints for paper
- Plastic rolling pins or cans
- Nonabsorbent flat surface for rolling out inks or paints (cookie sheets or wax paper)

How-to

1 Take a walk! Provide each child with a bag (labeled with his or her name) for storing leaves. (Back in the classroom, if children will be printing their leaves another day, have them store the leaves between sheets of waxed paper, and flatten with books or other weights. Leaves left out will curl and cannot be printed.)

2 Divide the class into small groups and provide each group with printing inks, rolling pins or cans, surfaces for rolling out ink, and cloth or paper squares. (You can limit your palette of inks and quilt squares to browns, gold, reds and oranges for an autumnal quilt, or show the whole year cycle with ink and quilt square colors selected for each season.)

3 Demonstrate how to use a rolling pin or can to roll out ink. Place a dollop of textile paint or water-based printing ink on a nonabsorbent surface. Roll the rolling pin (or can) through the paint or ink in several directions, spreading the color over the nonabsorbent surface and loading the pin or can with color for printing.

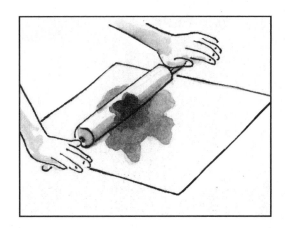

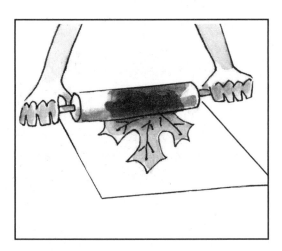

4 Place a leaf on a surface covered with newspaper. Roll the "loaded" rolling pin or can over the surface of a leaf. This will distribute color lightly and evenly over the surface of the leaf, highlighting the intricate vein structure. Carefully lift the leaf. Place the colored surface onto the quilt square and press all around to print. Carefully lift the leaf to reveal a realistic looking printed one!

5 Have each child print his or her square, then allow to dry completely. (If you are using textile paint and cloth, allow the paints to dry completely, and then iron the reverse side of the cloth to heat-set the color, making it permanent.) Save all the used leaves. Assemble the squares to form a quilt (see page 6).

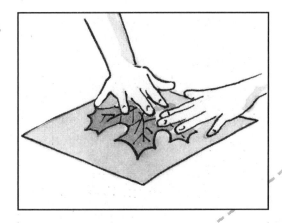

Book Links

The Fall of Freddie the Leaf: A Story of Life for All Ages by Leo F. Buscaglia (Holt Rinehart Winston, 1983)
A warm, wise, and simple story about a leaf named Freddie who changes with the seasons.

Look What I Did With a Leaf! by Morteza E. Sohi (Walker, 1993)
Gives directions on how to choose leaves for shapes and color, how to arrange them in animal forms, or natural scenes, and how to preserve the finished work of art.

Red Leaf, Yellow Leaf by Lois Ehlert (Harcourt, 1991)
A visually striking, informative, and accurate nonfiction narrative celebrating a child's pleasure in a sugar maple. Includes clear instructions for planting and caring for the tree.

6 Display your class quilt. Discuss the different shapes, colors and details. Examine the leaves used to make the prints and challenge children to match leaves to prints. How can they tell which leaf made which print?

Art Talk!

Printmaking
In this medium, artists transfer an image from an original source to another surface.

PATTERN QUILT

Children build patterning skills as they create strips of alternating shapes. As children add the strips layer upon layer, watch the patterns grow!

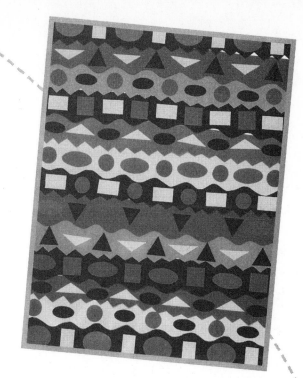

Set-up

■ Precut a strip of colored paper for each child. The sample above shows strips with a length of 18 inches and a width of 2½ inches. The strips can have straight edges, or for variety, use decorative scissors to create wavy or zigzag edges.

■ Precut lots of shapes that fit on the strips (see page 22 for reference) in different colors. Older children may wish to cut out their own shapes.

NOTE: Try limiting the color palette. You may wish to use primary colors, colors relating to a certain season or holiday, or a palette of black, white, and gray.

Materials

■ **Paper strip for each child (use three to five different colors in all)**

■ **Precut paper shapes (circles, semicircles, triangles, squares, ovals, rectangles, hexagons, diamonds and more; use the same palette of three to five colors)**

■ **Pencils**

■ **Scissors**

■ **Glue sticks or white glue**

How-to

1 Discuss what makes a pattern. Guide children to understand that a pattern is a repeating arrangement of colors or shapes. Clap out some AB patterns (clap hands together, put hands on lap, repeat several times). Together, examine patterns in books (see page 21 for suggestions).

2 Divide the class into groups and provide each group with paper strips, pattern shapes, and glue. (For older groups who can cut their own shapes, provide paper and scissors.)

3 Have children arrange two shapes of their choice in AB patterns on their strips. Then have them glue the shapes to the strips.

AB Pattern

4 Assemble children's completed pattern bars by stacking them, alternating the different colors. Attach bars to a stiff poster board, or staple them directly onto a bulletin board. For an added challenge, you might try more complicated patterns (ABC, ABBA, and so on)!

ABC Pattern

ABB Pattern

5 Invite children to share their quilt patterns and to find examples of other patterns in their environments. Create some rhythms by clapping and tapping out the whole quilt (for instance, for an ABAB pattern, you might clap, snap, clap, snap)!

Art Talk!

Pattern refers to the repetition of elements or of a motif.

Repetition appears when an art element occurs over and over, producing visual rhythm.

Rhythm is a principle of art in which the appearance of movement is created by the recurrence of elements.

Book Links

Lots and Lots of Zebra Stripes: Patterns in Nature by Stephen R. Swinburne (Boyds Mill Press, 1998) Stunning photographs invite kids to find patterns in such things as the ocean, ponds, spiderwebs, snake skins, fruits, and rocks.

Pattern (Math Counts) by Henry Pluckrose (Children's Press Art, 1995) Introduces children to the mathematical concept of pattern, and gives opportunities to find patterns in the world around them.

Patterns: What Comes Next by Michele Koomen (Bridgestone Books, 2001) Explains the concept of pattern in simple text, with real-life examples and color photographs and illustrations. Hands-on activities give opportunities for applying the concept.

What's Next, Nina? (Math Matters) by Sue Kassirer (Kane Press, 2001) Nina borrows a necklace from her sister without asking. It breaks and she has to reconstruct it—and in doing so, learns about patterns.

Shape Patterns

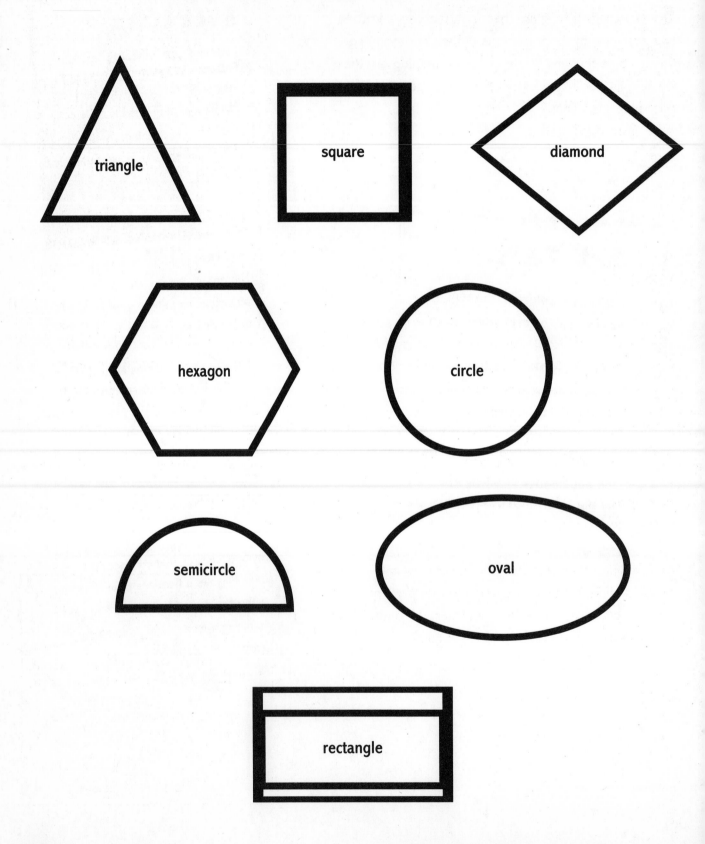

triangle

square

diamond

hexagon

circle

semicircle

oval

rectangle

TEXTURE QUILT

Children will sharpen their observation skills as they discover textures in the world around them.

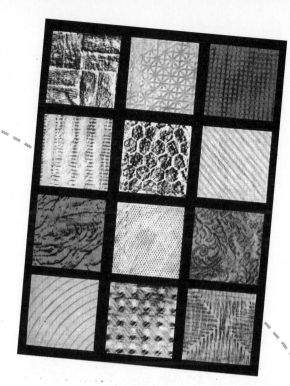

How-to

1 Discuss the concept of texture. *What is it? Where can you find textures?* Guide children to understand that texture is the look and feel of something, especially its roughness or smoothness. Look around the room and identify the many different textured surfaces such as linoleum, wood surfaces, brick walls, and so on. Use words to describe each one (*smooth, bumpy, scratchy,* and so on).

2 Provide each child with paper quilt squares, peeled crayons, scissors, and glue.

3 Demonstrate how to position paper over one of the textured surfaces you've identified in the room, hold it firmly in place with your hand, and with the other hand rub the side of the crayon over the paper.

Materials

- **Paper squares, three or four per child (use plain white paper or light-colored construction paper)**
- **Peeled crayons (dark colors are most effective)**

4 Children can collect rubbings from many surfaces, using one texture per paper, employing different colored papers and crayons for variety. Have children try to cover as much of the paper as possible with the rubbing.

5 Assemble the paper squares into a quilt (see page 6; you can first mount the texture squares onto larger construction paper squares if desired). Adhere to a stiff backing, or staple directly to a bulletin board.

6 Gather around the texture quilt and have a guessing game. For each square, ask children to guess where each texture was created.

Book Links

Feely Bugs by David A. Carter (Little Simon, 1995)
A touch-and-feel book to teach kids about textures.

How Artists Use Pattern and Texture by Paul Flux (Heinemann, 2001)
Explores different patterns that appear in art, and examines how patterns affect the viewer's perceptions of texture, depth, and shape.

Art Talk!

Texture is the surface quality or "feel" of an object (smooth, rough, soft). Textures may be actual (tactile, or felt by touch) or implied (suggested by the way an artist has created a work of art).

CONTRASTING SNOWFLAKES QUILT

Children explore the concepts of light and dark as they create a beautiful winter display.

How-to

1 Give each child scissors and four paper squares (two white, two colored). Have children begin by folding a white square in half. They bring one side across to meet the opposite side, matching the corners, and press down the center to crease. They then fold the doubled paper in half the other direction, and crease. Next, children fold the square into a triangle shape, and crease.

Materials

- White paper squares, two per child
- Colorful paper squares in different shades of blue, violet, and turquoise, two of the same color per child
- Scissors
- Glue

2 Demonstrate how to cut small shapes. Encourage children to try triangles, half hearts, semicircles and more, cutting through all the folds of the paper. Children can then open up the folded squares to reveal the snowflake patterns.

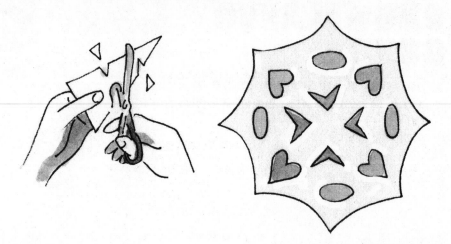

3 Show children how to glue the white snowflake onto the colored square. They then repeat the entire process, using the *colored* square for a snowflake and the *white* square for a background.

4 To assemble the quilt, alternate by background color: white, color, white, color. Adhere squares to a stiff board, or staple directly to a bulletin board (see page 6).

5 Gather the group around the quilt. Point out that just like real snowflakes, no two patterns are the same. Ask children to point to a light color, then a dark color. Explain that dark and light often look good together because they *contrast*, or are different from, each other.

Art Talk!

Contrast is the amount of darkness or brightness between colors.

There is **high contrast** when a dark and a light color are placed near each other.

There is **low contrast** when colors similar in value are placed near each other.

Positive space is the space occupied by a form or a shape (here, the snowflake).

Negative space is the background, or the empty space surrounding a positive space (here, the background).

Book Links

Snowflake Bentley by Jacqueline Briggs Martin (Houghton Mifflin, 1998)
Tells the story of Wilson Bentley, a young boy who loved snowflakes so much that he spent his whole life photographing the tiny ice crystals.

Snowflakes for All Seasons by Cindy Higham (Gibbs Smith, 2004)
A craft book for all ages with activities designed for every season.

PAPEL PICADO QUILT

Nothing says "fiesta" like color! Celebrate Cinco de Mayo or Dia de los Muertos with this easy folding and cutting project.

Materials

- 6-inch tissue paper squares in a variety of colors, several per child
- Scissors
- Child-safe pinking shears (scissors that make curvy or zigzag edges)
- Hole punches
- White background for display (bulletin board covered with white butcher paper, or white mounting board)

How-to

1 Divide the class into groups. Distribute hole punches, scissors, pinking shears, and tissue paper squares.

2 Show children how to fan-fold the tissue squares. Starting at one end, they make a fold about one inch deep. They then fold the paper back another inch in the opposite direction. Children keep folding back and forth until they have folded the entire square.

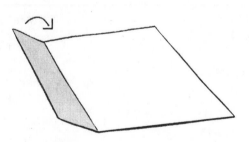
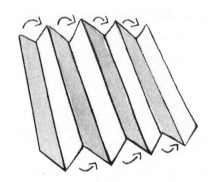

3 Show children how to use the hole punch, scissors, and pinking shears to punch and cut small simple shapes into the folds. They can then open up and flatten the folded square for the final *papel picado* (cut paper).

4 Encourage children to create more squares, experimenting with different decorative edges and varied shape cuts.

5 Assemble the *papel picado* squares into a quilt (see page 6). Attach them to the white background to show off their vibrant colors! Explain that this type of quilt uses bright, strong colors. Ask, *What is the opposite of bright?* Have children find examples of bright and dull objects in the room.

Art Talk!

Color is produced when light strikes an object and reflects back in your eyes. This element of art has three properties:

Hue is a variety of color (red, yellow, blue).

Intensity refers to the purity and strength of a color (bright red or dull red).

Value refers to the lightness or darkness of a color.

Book Links

Arts and Crafts of Mexico by Chloe Sayer and David Lavender (Chronicle Books, 1990)
Portrays Mexican cultures and folk art with color photographs, a guide to indigenous peoples, map, glossary, and bibliography.

Cinco de Mayo (World Holidays) by Sarah Vasquez (Raintree/Steck Vaughn, 1998)
Introduces the customs and practices of this Mexican holiday. Includes history, costumes, music, dances, parades, parties, foods, and activities.

Day of the Dead by Tony Johnston (Voyager Books, 2000)
Shares how a Mexican family celebrates this holiday. The covers, end papers, and title page are decorated with silhouettes similar to the cut-paper banners that beautify the home altars.

Mexican Papercutting: Simple Techniques for Creating Colorful Cut-Paper Projects by Kathleen Trenchard (Lark Books, 1998)
Contains detailed and easy-to-follow instructions on the art of paper cutting, with patterns for all levels.

BLACK, WHITE & READ ALL OVER QUILT

Weave together art and letter recognition! Children hunt through newspapers and magazines for upper and lowercase examples of an assigned alphabet letter, then collage their collection on a quilt block.

Materials

- 6-inch paper quilt squares cut from white construction paper, two per child
- Newspapers and magazines, at least one per child
- Newsprint and magazine pages cut into 2-inch squares, at least nine squares per child
- Pencils
- Scissors
- Glue sticks or white glue

How-to

1 Divide the class into small groups and distribute quilt squares, magazines, newspapers, scissors and glue sticks.

2 Assign each child a different letter of the alphabet. Have children look through newspapers and magazines for large examples of their assigned letter and cut them out.

3 Help children use glue sticks to glue their letters onto the squares.

4 For the second quilt square, put out the 2-inch squares so that children can select their own. They can then glue the squares onto their second quilt square to create "nine-patch" squares. Encourage them to experiment rotating text, alternating dark and light backgrounds of type to create patterns (see below).

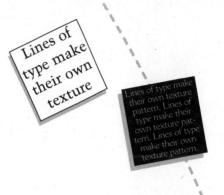

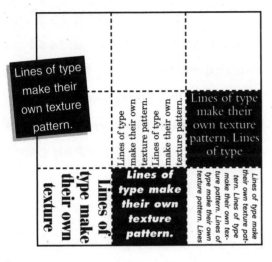

5 Assemble the quilt, alternating letter squares with the "nine-patch" squares. See page 6 for assembly tips.

6 Gather around and examine the quilt closely. Together, notice the many styles of each letter of the alphabet and the patterns printed type makes.

Book Links

Alphabet Affirmations: Positive Affirmations for Children by Bunny Hull (Brassheart Music, 2000)
Original songs, stories, and activity books that combine the ABCs with positive thoughts and self-affirmations.

Chicka Chicka Boom Boom by John Archambault (Little Simon, 1991)
In this rhythmic alphabet chant, all the letters of the alphabet race each other up the coconut tree!

Hands-On Alphabet Activities for Young Children: A Whole Language Plus Phonics Approach to Reading by Roberta Seckler Brown and Susan Carey (Jossey-Bass, 2002)
A great collection of stimulating, teacher-tested learning center activities that reinforce alphabet letters and their sounds.

Art Talk!

Collage is a piece of art created by gluing bits of paper, fabric, and so on to a flat surface.

Composition refers to the arrangement of the visual elements in a piece of art.

RECYCLED ENVELOPE QUILT CARDS

Patterns are all around us. Children will enjoy finding and collecting teeny-tiny patterns to create their own beautiful greeting cards.

Materials

- ■ Quilt cards (copies of page 34, one per child)
- ■ Business envelopes with a variety of decorative liners
- ■ Glue sticks or white glue

Set-up

Copy page 34 onto colored paper for each child. Precut 1" squares (so that each child can select nine from a large assortment) from a variety of patterned envelope liners. Older children might measure and cut their own squares.

How-to

1 Divide the class into groups. Have children fold their sheets of construction paper in half.

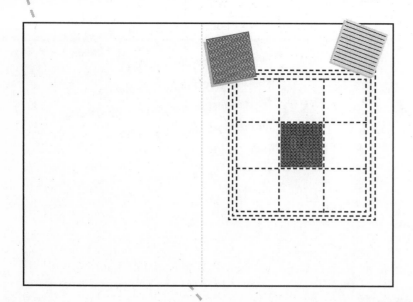

2 Explain that children will be creating miniature quilts on the front of their greeting cards. Invite children to examine the pattern squares and to explore different arrangements of their decorative squares. Explain that these quilts are in a "nine-patch" pattern because they have nine squares in rows of three. For an extra challenge, show children how to cut across the squares diagonally to form two triangles and have them try a quilt with triangle shapes:

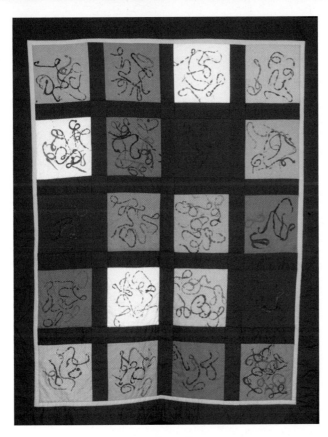

String Art Quilt pages 10–11

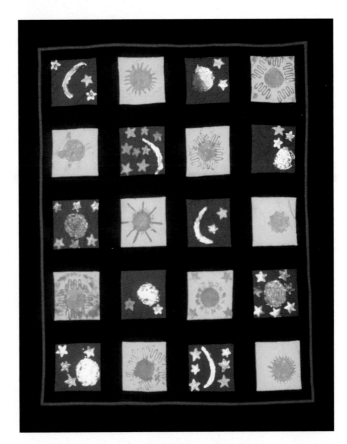

Sun, Moon & Stars Quilt pages 12–15

Leaf Print Quilt pages 16–18

Pattern Quilt pages 19–22

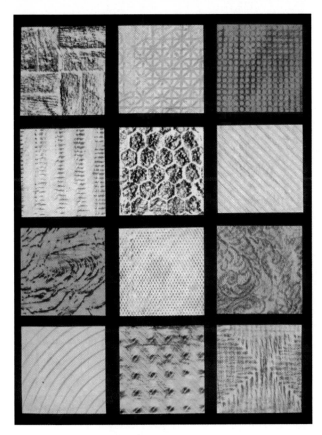

Texture Quilt pages 23–24

Contrasting Snowflakes Quilt pages 25–27

Papel Picado Quilt pages 28–29

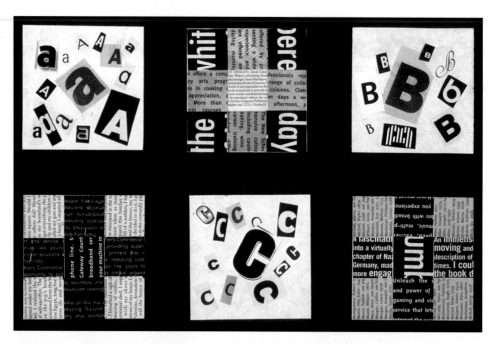

Black, White & Read All Over Quilt pages 30–31

Recycled Envelope Quilt Cards pages 32–34

Paper Weaving Quilt pages 35–37

3-D Box Quilt pages 38–40

Recycling Quilt pages 41–42

Neighborhood Quilt pages 43–44

Impression Quilt pages 45–47

Geometric Quilt pages 48–51

3 Once they have decided upon their patterns, have children glue the square pieces onto their cards.

4 Invite children to write a greeting inside the card and take it home to give to someone special.

Art Talk!

Harmony refers to the related qualities of the visual elements of a composition. Harmony is achieved by repetition of characteristics that are the same or similar.

Patchwork describes something composed of miscellaneous or incongruous parts (hodgepodge).

Book Links

Card Crafting: Over 45 Ideas for Making Greeting Cards & Stationary by Gillian Souter (Sterling, 1993)
Forty-five card and stationery designs in full color with complete and clear instructions and patterns.

Ecoart!: Earth-Friendly Art and Craft Experiences for 3- to 9-Year-Olds by Laurie Carlson (Williamson, 1992)
Great projects with clear, concise instructions. All projects use recyclable, reusable household materials or items found in nature.

Every Day Is Earth Day: A Craft Book by Kathy Ross (Millbrook, 1995)
Introduces the concept of recycling with comprehensive project ideas that encourage the re-use of everyday items.

Making Greeting Cards With Creative Materials by Maryjo McGraw (North Light, 2002)
Provides imaginative and artistic greeting card ideas from innovative materials.

The Seasons Sewn: A Year in Patchwork by Ann Whitford Paul (Harcourt, 1996)
The author explains 24 classic quilt patterns through stories. Each story is accompanied by photographs of the pattern and illustrations depicting life in the nineteenth century throughout the four seasons.

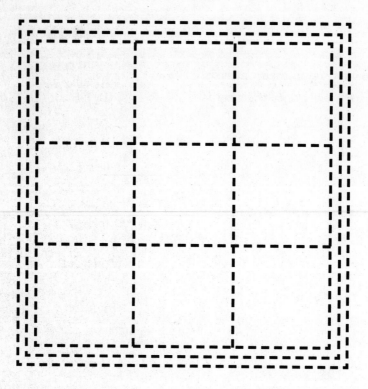

Made by _____

PAPER WEAVING QUILT

Paper weaving is a great way to teach patterning—and develop fine-motor skills at the same time!

How-to

1 Divide the class into groups. Provide each group with an assortment of colored construction paper squares, rulers, pencils, and scissors.

2 Have children select one colored square, fold it in half, and crease the fold.

3 Show children how to use the ruler to make cuts in the paper about an inch apart, from the folded edge close to the outer edge of the paper. Remind them not to cut through the edge. They can then open the papers and spread them flat.

Materials

- 7-inch squares of construction paper, one each of two different colors per child
- Rulers
- Pencils
- Scissors
- Glue sticks or white glue

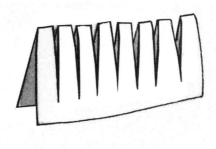

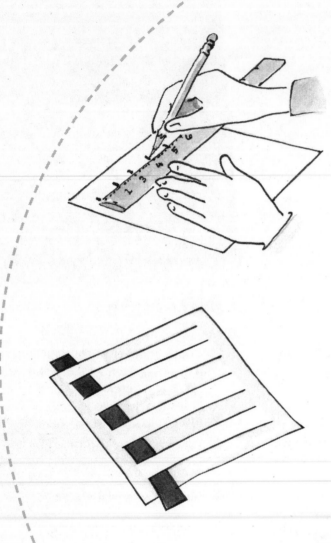

4 Have children choose a second square of colored paper, and use the ruler to mark off strips. The strips need not be perfect, but this gives children the opportunity for practice in measuring. Have them cut apart the strips. You can expand the palette to teach color concepts (such as primary and secondary colors: use red, blue, and purple to teach that red and blue make purple) or to celebrate a holiday or season!

5 Demonstrate how to weave the strips into the slits, first sliding over, then under. Weave the second strip beginning under, then over. Alternate each row until the strips have filled the paper. Have children slide strips close together as they work.

6 Have children glue the ends of the strips in place. Assemble the squares into a quilt (see page 6).

7 Display the collaborative weaving for all to see!

Art Talk!

Primary colors are red, yellow, and blue—the colors that are used to mix all other colors. No colors can be mixed to obtain primary colors.

Secondary colors are orange, green, and violet. These colors can each be mixed by combining two primary colors.

Book Links

Abuela's Weave by Omar S. Castañeda (Lee & Low Books, 1993)
Tells the story of Esperanza, a Guatemalan girl learning to weave with her grandmother.

Guatemala Rainbow by Gianni Vecchiato (Pomegranate, 1990)
Stunning photos portray Guatemalan people and their traditional woven textiles.

The Magic Weaver of Rugs: A Tale of the Navajo by Jerrie Oughton (Houghton Mifflin, 1994)
A charming legend about a mythical being who teaches the Navajo to weave for warmth and survival.

Songs From the Loom: A Navajo Girl Learns to Weave by Monty Roessel (Lerner Publications, 1995)
This full-color photo essay of an Arizona Navajo reservation shows each step of the rug-making process—shearing, carding, spinning, dyeing, and weaving.

3-D BOX QUILT

Children will love bringing their quilts into the "third dimension" as they construct with recyclables and found objects. There's also wonderful shadow play in the many raised and recessed surfaces!

Materials

- Shoeboxes (both lids and bottoms), one per child
- An assortment of small boxes (jewelry boxes, envelope boxes, and so on)
- 3-D recyclables such as paper towel rolls, egg cartons, plastic baskets, lids and caps from bottles and jars, foam peanuts, sculpted foam rubber, styrofoam peanuts, and more
- Scissors
- Glue
- Large cardboard backing
- White paint
- Paintbrushes

How-to

1 Share examples of sculptor Louise Nevelson's work (see box, page 39). This artist constructs 3-D elements in boxes, then assembles the boxes together and paints them a solid color.

2 Have each child choose a shoebox lid or bottom. Provide children with a variety of recycled materials and found objects, scissors, glue, and white paint. You may wish to have a discussion about recycling first.

Web sites

To find examples of Louise Nevelson's box sculptures, look for these images:

www.albrightknox.org/ArtStart/INevelson.html

www.bochum.de/museum/besitz04.htm

3 Encourage exploration and invention! Children can cut apart items and combine them in unusual ways. Have them arrange the materials in the boxes and glue the pieces to secure.

4 When the glue is dry, show children how to paint their box sculptures thoroughly with white paint. Allow paint to dry completely.

5 Assemble the boxes into a 3-D quilt! Staple them to a large bulletin board. Align box edges closely together. (Boxes will be easy to return to children when you take the exhibition down.)

6 Display the 3-D box quilt and experiment with different light sources. Turn the classroom lights off. Using a flashlight, move the light source to different angles. Ask children to describe what they see in different lighting situations. Try again with the lights on. Notice how light and shadow helps show off the different forms and space.

Book Links

Shadows by Carolyn B. Otto
(Scholastic Reference, 2001)
This science reader explains what shadows are and why they change—and provides fun flashlight experiments!

Shadowville by Michael Bartalos
(Viking, 1995)
A playful rhyming text and bold graphic illustrations explore the secret life of shadows.

Art Talk!

Form is the shape and structure of something.

Space is the area between and around objects.

RECYCLING QUILT

"One person's garbage is another's treasure." Here's a chance for kids to find potential in unwanted items—plus develop resourcefulness and flexible thinking.

Set-up

Precut 7-inch quilt squares (one per child) from manila envelopes, old cereal boxes, or cardboard. Punch holes in each corner and in the center edges. (You can adjust the settings on a three-hole punch to punch corners and center simultaneously.)

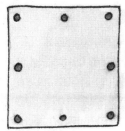 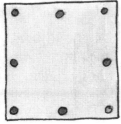

Materials

- Used manila folders, cereal boxes, or other recycled cardboard
- Child-safe recyclable materials such as metals (aluminum foil, bottle tops); plastics (plastic cutlery, lids, shallow containers); papers; corrugated cardboard; bubble wrap; and so on!
- Scissors
- White glue
- Hole punch
- Twist-ties (12 per child)

How-to

1 Divide the class into groups. Provide each group with cardboard squares, a variety of recycled materials, scissors, and glue.

2 Help children sort all the recycled materials into groups: plastic, metals, cardboard, and paper. Discuss recycling as a way of taking care of the Earth. Explain that it is a way to reuse things and create less garbage.

3 Ask each child to select a category and create his or her square with items from that group. Children arrange the items on their squares then glue them to the cardboard square. Let dry completely.

4 Assemble the squares into a quilt, alternating categories of recycled materials, using twist-ties through the holes.

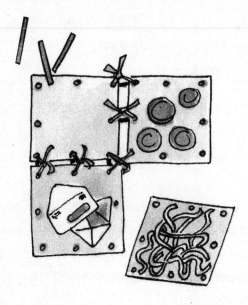

5 Display your quilt with a title such as "We Recycle"!

Book Links

50 Simple Things Kids Can Do to Recycle by Earthworks Group (Bathroom Readers, 1994)
This book provides projects and activities that help children to implement recycling at home, in their community, and at school.

Recycle: A Handbook for Kids by Gail Gibbons (Little Brown & Co, 1996)
Explains exactly how an item gets recycled.

Recycle That! by Fay Robinson and Allan Fowler (Children's Press, 1995)
Describes the effects of trash, and how trash can be recycled.

Earth Book for Kids: Activities to Help Heal the Environment by Linda Schwartz (Learning Works, 1990)
This book is full of ideas for arts and crafts projects, experiments, and experiences.

Art Talk!

Variety creates interest in a composition by opposing, contrasting, changing, elaborating, or diversifying the elements.

NEIGHBORHOOD QUILT

Kids create a quilt that is also a grid of city blocks! Here's a great way to enrich your study of neighborhoods and communities.

How-to

1 Take children on a neighborhood walk and point out buildings that meet our needs: shelter (homes), food (restaurant), health (hospital), safety (firehouse), education (school), government (town hall), entertainment (movie theater) and so on.

2 Back in the classroom, make a list of the buildings you saw. Have each child select a different type of building for his or her quilt square.

3 Divide the class into groups and give each child a paper square. Provide each group with pencils, markers, and crayons.

4 Have children draw their buildings on their quilt squares.

Materials

- 7-inch squares of white drawing paper, one per child
- Black background paper for bulletin board
- Yellow paint
- Paintbrush
- Pencils
- Markers, crayons, or colored pencils

Book Links

All Around Town: Exploring Your Community Through Craft Fun
by Judy Press (Williamson, 2002)
A great resource of activities on the theme of neighborhood.

Cassie's Word Quilt by Faith Ringgold
(Knopf, 2002)
A young girl takes early readers on a tour of her 1930s-era Harlem home, school, and neighborhood.

On the Town: A Community Adventure
by Judith Caseley (Greenwillow, 2002)
A homework assignment sends Charlie and his mother exploring their community. Charlie's lively notebook entries "illustrate" their adventure.

5 Staple squares in a grid pattern directly to a bulletin board covered in black paper, allowing some paper to frame the squares like a grid of streets. Have a child help you create traffic lines on the "streets" with yellow paint.

6 A neighborhood is born! Invite children to write a description of their new community.

Art Talk!

Unity is the feeling of harmony between all parts of an artwork, creating a sense of completeness.

IMPRESSION QUILT

Cook your own play dough for an interesting quilt. Kids love rolling it out and pressing in found objects to create textured tiles!

Set-up

Make, enough play dough for each child to roll out a tile (recipe on page 47 makes eight tiles).

How-to

1 Divide the class into small groups and provide each child with play dough. Provide each group with rolling pins, cardboard square, plastic knives, pencils, or pens for creating corner holes, and objects for making impressions.

2 With the rolling pin, demonstrate how to roll out a flat, even slab of dough or clay. Have children roll their own sheets.

Materials

- 4-inch cardboard square, one per group
- Play dough (see recipe, page 47)
- Rolling pins, one per child
- Plastic knives, one per child
- An assortment of materials for making impressions (nuts, bolts, paper clips, screws, craft sticks, straws, puzzle pieces, blocks, buttons, jacks, clothes pins, cookie cutters, coins, bottle tops, dry pasta, beans, pebbles, small toys, forks, spoons, keys, string, pine cones, leaves, jewelry, and so on)
- Pencil or pens for creating corner holes
- Long straight pins (four per square)

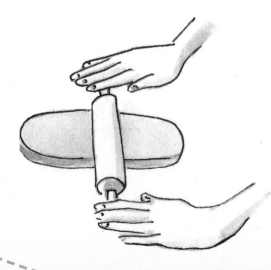

Art Talk!

A **slab** is a mass of wet clay flattened to a sheet with a rolling pin.

Book Links

Create Anything With Clay
by Sherri Haab (Klutz, 1999)
Comes with eight blocks of colorful polymer clay and a wide variety of project ideas.

Feeling Things by Allan Fowler
(Children's Press, 1991)
Discusses the sense of touch and how it works to tell us more about the world around us.

Mudworks: Creative Clay, Dough, and Modeling Experiences by MaryAnn F. Kohl (Bright Ring, 1992)
Includes more than 100 recipes for dough, plaster, clay, and other modeling mixtures, plus numerous activities.

Play-Doh Art Projects by Kathy Ross
(Millbrook, 2002)
Offers a variety of projects using Play-Doh and a few simple household items.

3 Have children position the quilt square templates on the dough and cut around the edges with the plastic knife to create the tile.

4 Invite children to press various objects into the soft tiles to make impressions. While the dough is still moist, have children create a small hole in each corner (for later display).

5 Leave to dry overnight. Flip the tiles over once to expose the underside to air. Again, leave to dry overnight until the tiles dry thoroughly on each side.

6 Assemble tiles into a quilt by pinning them onto a bulletin board through the holes in each corner. (Later, children can take their tiles home.)

7 Gather around the assembled quilt. Notice the play of lights and shadows on the impressions. Ask children to guess how different textures were made. Then, have children close their eyes and feel the imprints, trying to guess what object created each.

PLAY DOUGH

2 cups flour

1 cup salt

2 cups water

4 teaspoons cream of tartar

4 tablespoons cooking oil

Mix ingredients in a large saucepan. Cook over low heat (supervise children closely), stirring constantly until mixture comes away from the sides. Cool before using. Store in a tightly sealed container. Makes eight tiles.

4-inch SQUARE TEMPLATE
Use this template to cut out tiles.

GEOMETRIC QUILT

Some Muslim artists create beautiful designs using geometric shapes. Children will enjoy making designs and patterns with simple squares, triangles, and trapezoids of various colors.

Materials

- **2¼-inch quilt squares templates, one per child**
- **4½" quilt square base, one per child**
- **Shape templates: 1- and 1½-inch squares, triangles, and trapezoids (see patterns on page 51), one of each per child**
- **Colored papers**
- **Pencils**
- **Scissors**
- **Glue sticks**
- **Poster board or recycled manila folders**

Set-up

Precut 2¼-inch quilt squares, 4½-inch quilt square base, and shape templates for each child (page 51).

How-to

1 Share examples of Islamic geometric design (see page 50 for book suggestions): tiles, mosaics in architecture, carved designs on furniture, doors, walls, and boxes.

2 Divide the class into groups. Distribute quilt squares, quilt square bases, and shapes. Provide each group with an assortment of colored paper, pencils, scissors, and glue sticks.

3 Have children trace the 2¼-inch quilt square template onto the poster board four times, then cut out the pieces.

4 Help children trace the shape templates onto colored paper and cut out the colored shapes. Encourage children to experiment arranging the different colored shapes on the first of their squares.

5 When children have created designs they like, they can adhere the shapes to the background with a glue stick. The designs will grow into patterns when children repeat and vary the orientation of the squares by rotation.

6 Help children repeat the design three more times, for a total of four identical 2¼-inch quilt squares.

7 Have children position the four 2¼-inch quilt squares on the 4½-inch quilt base. They should not attach them yet. Encourage them to explore different ways of arranging the small squares to create a larger pattern, rotating and flopping the designs. When children have achieved a pleasing pattern, have them adhere the four squares to the quilt back.

All the patterns below are formed from different arrangements of the same 2½-inch square:

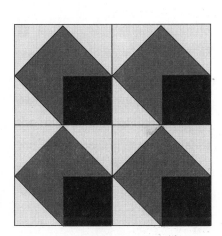

straight repeat

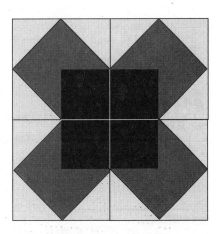

rotate toward center

rotate toward outside

Book Links

How Artists Use Shape by Paul Flux
(Heinemann, 2001)
Explains how artists create shapes
and how they use specific shape
combinations to portray an image or
a mood.

**Islamic Art in Context: Art,
Architecture, and the Literary World**
by Robert Irwin (Harry N. Abrams, 1997)
Surveys the Islamic culture and arts of
painting, architecture, porcelain, enamel,
manuscript illumination, metalwork,
calligraphy, textiles, and more.

Islamic Ornament by Eva Baer
(New York University Press, 1998)
A in-depth study of the history,
function, and significance of ornament
in Islamic art.

8 Assemble the four-block quilt
squares into a larger classroom quilt.
(see page 6 for tips). Watch the
patterns grow!

9 Have children identify patterns
and describe how they repeated and
varied their patterns.

Art Talk!

Shape is a two-dimensional area
or plane that may be free-form or
geometric, open or closed, natural
or manufactured.

4½-inch QUILT SQUARE
Attach the four smaller squares to this base.

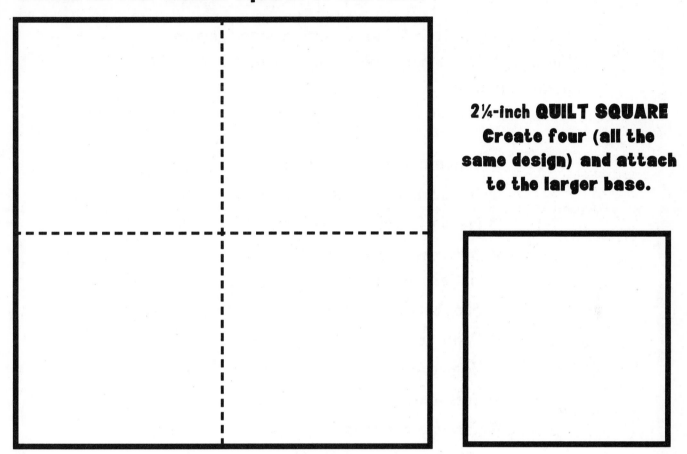

2¼-inch QUILT SQUARE
Create four (all the same design) and attach to the larger base.

SHAPE TEMPLATES
Cut shapes in various colors.

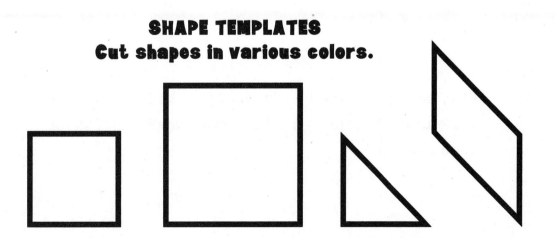

Dear Families,

We have many fun quilting projects planned this year. Please help us gather materials by saving the following items at home and bringing them to our classroom. Encourage creative recycling!

- **Construction paper scraps**
- **Magazines & newspapers**
- **Manila folders & envelopes**
- **Business envelopes with printed patterned interiors**
- **Shoeboxes**
- **Paper towel rolls**
- **Egg cartons**
- **Twist-ties**
- **Cardboard scraps**
- **Styrofoam trays & packing "peanuts"**
- **Leaves**
- **String**
- **Buttons**
- **Keys**

Also, please feel free to join us in the classroom and help with our quilt projects. We have many opportunities for adult helpers!

Sincerely,

Quilt Snack

Celebrate your work with a square snack!

TOASTED QUILT SQUARES

Ingredients (one of each per child)

- slice of bread
- square of white cheese (individually wrapped slice)
- square of yellow cheese (individually wrapped slice)

Materials

- large baking sheet
- plastic knives
- small shaped cookie cutters
- convection, conventional, or toaster oven (for adult use only)
- paper plates, one per child

Directions

1. Place the bread on the baking sheet.

2. Tear the cheese into squares or use knives or cookie cutters to make shapes. Make a design or pattern on the bread.

3. Toast to melt the cheese.

4. Cool and eat.

Quilting Games, Activities & Teaching Tools

Create new quilts—or use old ones for something new!

Alphabet Quilt

Create an interactive quilt from a pocket chart. Letter the pockets from A to Z. Place small objects or toys inside each pocket, from alligators to zebras. Or, use transparent pockets to showcase kids' alphabet drawings.

Calendar Quilt

If you use a calendar pocket chart, turn it into a quilt by substituting squares upon which children have drawn.

Checkers, Chess, or Backgammon Quilt

Familiar board games make great templates for quilts. Use regular game pieces, soft-sculpted ones that stick with Velcro, felt, old buttons, or even small candies!

Coloring Blocks

Find printable coloring pages for a large variety of traditional block patterns at http://blockcentral.com/coloringbook.shtml

Block Quilt

Have children use blocks of different shapes and colors to create a quilt on the floor in the block area!

Creative Writing

Show and tell with quilts brought from home. Use sharing as a springboard for creative writing. Who made the quilt and why?

Dramatic Play

Have a classroom discussion about quilts, how comforting they are, and how warm they keep you. Have each child pretend to be under a warm snuggly quilt. Put a quilt in the dramatic play center!

Graphs and Ratios

Use a quilt brought in from home or one created in class. How many red squares? yellow? green? Make bar charts. Discuss how many pieces make a whole.

I Spy

Play I Spy while looking at a quilt. Children love looking for colors, shapes, and recognizable objects.

Memory Game

Create an interactive quilt with picture pairs underneath flaps that children can discover and match up.

Post Office

Use envelope pockets labeled for each child on individual quilt squares and create an interactive classoom postal station. Children can open their mailbox to find letters and postcards inside.

Tic-Tac-Toe

Use a nine-patch quilt with Velcro game pieces or bean bags that can be tossed at a jumbo quilt for an added challenge.

Quilt Museums

Follow up your study of quilts with a museum visit—in person or online!

Hanford Mills Museum
P.O. Box 99
East Meredith, NY 13757
http://www.hanfordmills.org/museum.htm

La Conner Quilt Museum
703 S. 2nd Street
La Conner, WA 98257
http://www.laconnerquilts.com/index.html

Museum of the American Quilter's Society
215 Jefferson Street
Paducah, KY 42001
http://www.quiltmuseum.org/index.html

Museum of Florida History
500 South Bronough Street
Tallahassee, FL 32399
http://dhr.dos.state.fl.us/museum

The New England Quilt Museum
18 Shattuck Street
Lowell, MA 01852
http://www.nequiltmuseum.org

The People's Place Quilt Museum
3510 Old Philadelphia Pike
P.O. Box 419
Intercourse, PA 17534
http://www.800padutch.com/z/ppquiltmuseum.htm

The Quilters Hall of Fame
926 Washington St.
Marion, IN 46953
http://www.quiltershalloffame.org

The Rocky Mountain Quilt Museum
1111 Washington Avenue
Golden, CO 80401
http://www.rmqm.org/html/links.html

San Jose Museum of Quilts & Textiles
110 Paseo de San Antonio
San Jose, CA 95112
http://www.sjquiltmuseum.org

Virginia Quilt Museum
301 South Main Street
Harrisonburg, VA 22801
http://www.vcq.org/museums.htm

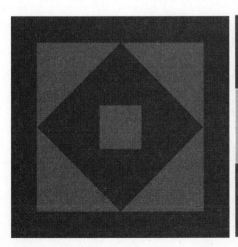

Community Service Opportunities

If you've made durable cloth quilts, consider donating them to a worthy cause!

ABC Quilts gives love and comfort to at-risk babies in the form of a handmade quilt, and uses process to promote awareness, community service, and prevention education.
http://abcquilts.org/home.html

Binky Patrol distributes handmade blankets to children who are sick, abused, or in foster care.
http://www.binkypatrol.org

Hugs for Homeless Animals, Snuggles Project provides handmade blankets and quilts to comfort animals in shelters.
http://www.h4ha.org/snuggles

Project Linus is a nonprofit organization that makes handmade blankets and quilts for children in need. There are local chapters all over the country.
http://www.projectlinus.org

Quilts for Kids transforms discontinued fabrics into quilts that comfort children in crisis.
11 Effingham Road
Yardley, PA 19067
http://www.quiltsforkids.org

Warming Families is a crafting project designed to get all members of the family involved in helping provide needed blankets for homeless families.
http://www.warmingfamilies.org

Wrap Them in Love collects donated quilts and distributes them to children around the world so they can be wrapped in the love of a quilt.
401 N. Olympic Ave.
Arlington, WA 98223
http://www.wraptheminlove.org

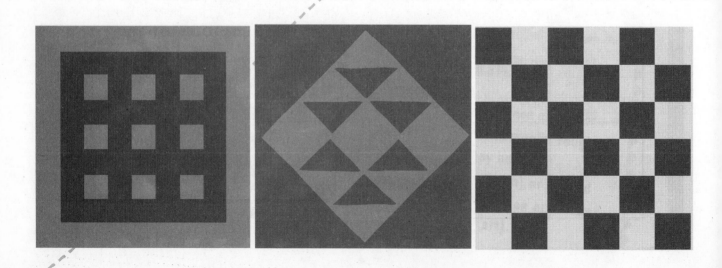

Quilting Bibliography

Picture Books

Eight Hands Round: A Patchwork Alphabet
by Ann Whitford Paul (HarperTrophy, 1996)

The Josephina Story Quilt
by Eleanor Coerr (HarperCollins, 1986)

The Keeping Quilt
by Patricia Polacco (Simon & Schuster, 1998)

The Log Cabin Quilt
by Ellen Howard (Holiday House, 1996)

The Name Quilt
by Phyllis Root (Farrar, Straus & Giroux, 2003)

Oma's Quilt
by Paulette Bourgeois (Kids Can Press, 2001)

The Quilt
by Ann Jonas (Puffin, 1994)

Quilt of Dreams
by Mindy Dwyer (Alaska Northwest Books, 2000)

The Quilt Story
by Tony Johnston (Puffin, 1996)

Sam Johnson and the Blue Ribbon Quilt
by Lisa Campbell Ernst (HarperTrophy, 1992)

Selina and the Bear Paw Quilt
by Barbara Smucker (Knopf, 1996)

Tar Beach
by Faith Ringgold (Crown, 1991)

Texas Star
by Barbara Hancock Cole (Orchard, 1990)

The Tortilla Quilt
by Jane Tenorio-Coscarelli (Quarter Inch, 1996)

Activity Books

Creative Quilting With Kids
by Maggie Ball and Mark Frey (Krause, 2001)

Easy Literature-Based Quilts Around the Year (Grades K–3) by Mariann Cigrand and Phyllis Howard (Scholastic, 2000)

Kids Can Quilt: Fun and Easy Projects for Your Small Quilter by Dorothy Stapleton (Barrons, 2004)

Kids Easy Quilting Projects (Quick Starts for Kids!) by Terri Thibault, Heather Barberie, Beth Hoffman, and Peg Blanchette (Williamson Publishing, 2001)

Month-by-Month Quilt and Learn Activities: 25 Easy, No-Sew Quilting Activities for Reading, Writing, Math, Social Studies, and More by Kathy Pike, Jean Mumper, and Alice Fiske (Scholastic, 2002)

Quilting Activities Across the Curriculum (Grades 1–3) by Wendy Buchberg (Scholastic, 1999)

Traditional Quilts for Kids to Make
by Barbara J. Eikmeier
(That Patchwork Place, 2001)

Continued

Thematic Books

Amish Quilts

Reuben and the Quilt
by Merle Good (Good Books, 1999)

Amish Quilting Patterns: 56 Full-Size Ready-To-Use Design and Complete Instructions by Gwen Marston and Joe Cunningham (Dover, 1987)

Hawaiian & Native American Quilts

Luka's Quilt
by George Guback (Greenwillow, 1994)

To Honor and Comfort: Native Quilting Traditions by Michigan State University, Marsha MacDowell, and C. Kurt Dewhurst (Museum of New Mexico, 1997)

Native American Designs for Quilting by Joyce Mori (American Quilter's Society, 1998)

Holiday & Seasonal Quilts

The Seasons Sewn: A Year in Patchwork
by Ann Whitford Paul (Harcourt, 1996)

Happy Holiday Quilting by Sandra Hatch and Jeanne Stauffer (Houses of White Birches, 1998)

Math Quilts

Optical Illusions for Quilters
by Karen Combs (American Quilter's Society, 1997)

Pioneer Quilts

American Quilt-Making: Stories in Cloth
by Ann Stalcup (Powerkids Pr, 2003)

Quilting Now & Then
by Karen B. Willing and Julie B. Dock (Now & Then, 1994)

Quilt Block History of Pioneer Days
by Mary Cobb (Millbrook Press, 1995)

The Quilting Bee
by Gail Gibbons (HarperCollins, 2004)

Underground Railroad Quilts

Hidden in Plain View: A Secret Story of Quilts and the Underground Railroad by Raymond G. Dobard and Jacqueline L. Tobin (Doubleday, 1999)

Slave Quilts From the Antebellum South
by Gladys-Marie Fry (The University of North Carolina Press, 2002)

Sweet Clara and the Freedom Quilt
by Deborah Hopkinson (Dragonfly, 1995)

Under the Quilt of Night
by Deborah Hopkinson (Atheneum, 2002)

Aunt Harriet's Underground Railroad in the Sky
by Faith Ringgold (Dragonfly, 1995)

The Secret to Freedom
by Marcia K. Vaughan (Lee & Low Books, 2001)

Web Sites

http://www.aghines.com/Quilt/Lessonplans/lessonlinks.htm

Includes great links to sites using quilts and quilting in the classroom.

http://www.carolhurst.com/subjects/quilts.html

Picture books with a quilt theme are discussed on this site.

http://www.thecraftstudio.com/qwc/index.htm

This site has great ideas, techniques, and resources for quilting with children.

http://www.kathimitchell.com/quilt/quilt3.html

Provides links to historical references on quilts.

http://www.learner.org/teacherslab/math/geometry/shape/quilts

This site explores shape and symmetry in math through quilt activities.

http://members.aol.com/mathquilt

The MathQuilt web page provides a showcase for quilters around the world who find inspiration from the colorful world of tessellations, geometry, perspective, and fractals.

http://www.quiltethnic.com/lessonplans.html

Quilting lesson plans from an ethnic perspective are available on this site.

Art Talk!

A glossary of the definitions found throughout the book

Abstract Expressionism is a style in which the artist expresses a feeling or idea with form, line, or color, without having a representational subject matter.

Collage is a piece of art created by gluing bits of paper, fabric, and so on to a flat surface.

Color is produced when light strikes an object and reflects back in your eyes.

Composition refers to the arrangement of the visual elements in a piece of art.

Contrast is the amount of darkness or brightness between colors.

> There is **high contrast** when a dark and a light color are placed near each other.

> There is **low contrast** when colors similar in value are placed near each other.

Cool colors are on one half of the color wheel, from green to blue to violet.

Form is the shape and structure of something.

Harmony refers to the related qualities of the visual elements of a composition. Harmony is achieved by repetition of characteristics that are the same or similar.

Hue is a variety of color (red, yellow, blue).

Intensity refers to the purity and strength of a color (bright red or dull red).

Line is the path of a moving point through space, or a continuous mark. It can vary by length, width, texture, direction, and curve.

Movement refers to the path the viewer's eye takes through the artwork. It can be directed along lines, edges, shapes, and colors within the artwork.

Negative space is the background, or the empty space surrounding a positive space.

Patchwork describes something composed of miscellaneous or incongruous parts (hodgepodge).

Pattern refers to the repetition of elements or of a motif.

Positive space is the space occupied by a form or a shape.

Art Talk!

Primary colors are red, yellow, and blue—the colors that are used to mix all other colors. No colors can be mixed to obtain primary colors.

Printmaking is a medium where artists transfer an image from an original source to another surface.

Repetition occurs when an art element is repeated over and over, producing visual rhythm.

Rhythm is a principle of art in which the appearance of movement is created by the recurrence of elements.

Secondary colors are orange, green, and violet. These colors can each be mixed by combining two primary colors.

Shape is a two-dimensional area or plane that may be free-form or geometric, open or closed, natural or manufactured.

Slab A mass of wet clay flattened to a sheet with a rolling pin.

Space is the area between and around objects.

Texture is the surface quality or "feel" of an object (smooth, rough, soft). Textures may be actual (tactile, or felt by touch) or implied (suggested by the way an artist has created a work of art).

Value refers to the lightness or darkness of a color.

Variety creates interest in a composition by opposing, contrasting, changing, elaborating, or diversifying the elements.

Unity is the feeling of harmony between all parts a piece of art, creating a sense of completeness.

Warm colors are the half of the color wheel from yellow to orange to red.

Notes

Notes